Ten Swansea Writers

Talisman Arts Group

Poetry   Prose   Art

Editor-Publishers:
Talisman Arts Group
Swansea
South Wales

www.talismanartsgroup.com
talismanartsgroup@gmail.com

First Edition

* refers reader to the glossary on page 110

* refers reader to the glossary on page 110

Introduction

Early in 2014 some of us started to go to a poetry and writing group. We were mostly new to the already-busy writing world of Swansea but wanted to set up something that was a bit less hectic, to add to rather than compete with other established groups.

We chose a coffee bar rather than a pub and decided we were going to try to give a platform to writers who had not had many previous opportunities to read their work at length. The first evening was attended by only a handful of people but gradually numbers increased to the point where it was becoming difficult to fit in all the people vying for reading slots. A second evening a month was introduced, feature readers added and Talisman Poetry was properly established.

This anthology is aimed at bringing samples of ten of the Talisman writers to the general reading public. We believe that its strength lies in expressing a very wide range of approaches, interests, ideas and styles.

Talisman Poetry meets at Tino's Coffee Bar in Wind Street, Swansea on the first and last Wednesday evenings of each month, starting at eight and finishing at ten. You are always guaranteed a warm welcome as either a reader or as a listener. If you are not sure, just try it.

David Churchill
Host of Talisman Poetry

June 2016

Michael grew up in Senegal, West Africa and now lives in Swansea. He is a performing poet who started writing poetry when in University studying medicine.

Outside of writing, he splits his time between life as a GP in Swansea and working as a tropical medicine doctor in Sierra Leone, West Africa.

His poetry is an exploration of the tensions of living among many worlds simultaneously and his writing often drifts into both the natural and supernatural to achieve this.
His work has been described as surreal and imagistic, with touches of Sylvia Plath and TS Eliott.

Alongside his poetry, Michael is a columnist for the magazine Junior DR, writes commentaries on film and media for the British Journal of General Practice and has published multiple pieces online.

Michael Bryant

Octopus

If you made the octopus,
You would name the tentacles home,
Or work, or poetry or a daughter,
You would lengthen them with your nose,
So they could explore…
Yet retreat when they touch hard edges,
Shy hermit crabs,
Drawn in by your loving designs.

If I made an octopus,
Her eyes would record your eight dimensions,
Then wrap each one around you,
So that her suckers kept you safe.

But if we worked together,
The poor creature would be yet more confused,
I would bend a tentacle left, you right,
They would criss-cross and wrestle,
One would tear tentacles from limbs,
Another would sucker life,
Swelling purple with frustrated angst.

You would paint joy's smile,
Over my ferocious scowls,
Schizophrenia's tsunami,
Would tear her mind from memory,
So one tentacle would play a violin,
And be hit by another's drumstick,
While two arms that dare hold an ancient pen,
Will be crushed by digital prostheses.

So perhaps we should leave nature to her angels,
Save our threads from tangling,

I'll let the waves steal you,
From my thought's toxic corral,
Leave behind tentacles that bind,
Us to forsaken suckers of romance,
And I'll admire your colours unspoilt.

Poked

He clapped, and you jumped,
He poked, so you opened,
Because that's what they all said you should do,
Your elders coaxed, your grandmothers begged,
Grey beards and puyo wine their forceps,
Their voices echoed thunder's threat.

He poked your poverty,
Left your choice circumcised,
Deforested by convenient nuptial arrangements,
Numbed by a rusted iron uniform,
Until he dug out your most precious gift,
And raised her on a stake for a community's healing.

Then he jabbed your children,
Vaccinated them with bigoted doctrine,
Your sons acquiesced to ant colonies marching,
Your daughters hauled twice their weight in dry sticks.

When they grew strong,
He scoured your stain from his rainbow,
Flushed your purity in his crimson whirlpool,
And left you free of their trust.

Michael Bryant

When you poked through cracked savannah soil,
Your protesting arms were lonelier than dry trees,
Raised in a desperate drowning rave,
Only to be rebuked by winds of hierarchy,
And scorched by sons of convention.

Even when your leaks were stopped,
Your cradle restored to its nurturing glory,
You were remoulded to fit expectations,
Your blossoming choices conceived within,
Yet birthed in a frightened, constricted pupil,

And released through misogyny's contracting canal.

So you still feel his poke,
In every wary glance,
Under each locally-stacked deal,
While behind paralysed wide eyes,
You beg thunder to shatter,
Straw ceilings and iron-roofed regimes.

You plead for rain to fuel vines,
To strangle excuses of culture.

You cry droplets that birth fresh forests,
To shield your daughters from violation.

Towers of the Coed *

The towers of the Coed are hunting,
Her windows snarling eyes,
Set in solid brick heads heavy,
With an afro of depressed clouds,
They scour the town for any frailty.

Her wards swirling tentacles,
Enwrapping towns, families, villages,
And you.
In her hypodermic vortex.

Her fiery tongue of grass rolls out,
Covering towns too innocent,
And minds all too experienced alike,
In her smoky blanket.

Now the towers are marching,
Carried by feet shackled by section papers,
Driven your way by a hive mind,
Stalking ghosts of imagination,
Down twisted, distorted streets.

Your fear knows,
What your wandering synapses cannot,
That once inside the towers, doors open only one way,
A fly trap with a single ticket,
To Venus promises unfulfilled.

So you - you swam closer to her tentacles,
The towers' eyes ever on you,
Your arms raised in celebration,

In desperation, then resignation,
As her mouth opened,
Then became a clam.

And you were forever her hidden pearl.

Swaddling cloth

So, so still,
All has ceased,
Final surrender,
Like damp after thunder.

Lonely final breath blown,
A faint plaintive pained whistle,
Through mist swept from desert eyes,
Down into her sepulchral mouth.

Fingers that barely knew to grasp,
Held in a firm parody of hope,
Dough ball hands that rise no more,
Wrinkles rush through a release.

These callous tin man legs,
I washed over, you stirred,
Now mere seaweed washed up,

Still tiny limbs deafen my eyes.

Below we suffer your memory,
Images entombed, enshrined,
Yet my impatient time moves on,

A formal earthly trudge,
Roots graft around my feet,
I am mired in today's eternity.

Yet how you dance,
With souls free from lead,
Twirling playfully around Holy feet,

Buoyant butterflies about a bouquet,
Withheld from raining effluent,
Sheltered under a thorny crown.

Our wingless saviour

Unseen creator,
She was chosen before their time dawned,
Brightest, fastest among heaven's wings,
She chose to fall among her creation.

She cast aside flight's pretentions,
Burrowing deeper, she became one,
With a prince, then her own people,
And finally, merged beneath earth's mound.
She was chosen for a strange honour,
Surrounded by suitors and concubines,
Their passing feelers palm branches,
Held out desperate for Easter's hope.

She was chosen to outlive them all,
Her body now a stretched parody,
Of her lifespan, endless in phases,
Each breath pupating desperation.

Michael Bryant

Until she pulsates alone,
While pickled heads jostle,
Their feet headlamps burrowing,
To escape her crucified body.

Her babies crave the sky's glory
Becoming petulant prodigals,

Each roaming as they think best,
Hiding their chaos in activity,
They flee the uniform honeycomb,

Their wings privilege, above the drones,
Free from patrolling soldiers,
Controlling the mound's borg cube kingdom.

Dirt walls and soldiers sever,
Their lifeline to a fading source,
Now anguished by her slavery,
And exhausted by her reproduction.

Yet at last she births… change,

In a child, with wings crimson and face of light,
She carries her mother's deity,
She rises, shattering the sun-baked mound,
Bursting the mud barricades,
Beating claws into ploughshares,

She is raised up above convention,
To transcend each mound kingdom.

Wrath redeemed

Can fire stand forever?
Her excited sparkles dance eternally,
When snow surges over each hill?
Where ice is a spreading bald patch,
Over a moribund intellect,
Victim to time's cold disdain?

I saw a fire fall into the sea,
Swallowed like Jonah by every wave,
Its dying breath sprayed up in steam,
Surrendered to straight-laced order.

I smelt smoke from where fire burned,
Yet the ground was painted with litter,
Cracked mirrors, antennae and coiled telephone wire,
Vanity strangled the last lonely flicker.

In a picture of Hiroshima,
I saw a devouring fire,
That could not be quenched,
And I wondered if He walked there.

I heard a furnace scream,
Through a mother's wail,
Over a baby's final deliverance,
So I knew our vengeance was not His fire.
I heard, "Take off your shoes",
We dared lay down my leaden soul,
Took on sandals of peace,
And a lamb carried His fire across the red sea.

Michael Bryant

Sighs

She returns,
Poker faced blanket stares back,
One less plate at the table,
Reverse musical chairs.

Returns to where he played,
Breeze blows the bells over,
Ball rolls over cold sand,
Topples to a forgotten corner.

Mummy's music plays to a vacant hall,
Big sister wakens to one less cry,
Daddy worries a little less,
Wishes he could feel his fruit near his loins,
His sadness besieged behind his eyes.

A home sighs,
Her mud walls sagging with cares,
Father puts iron protection around her,
Holds his spade across his chest,
Mother sets up another iron pot,
Squashes the flames underfoot.

David Churchill

David was born in Swansea, close to where the river Tawe meets the sea.

He is a poetry and prose writer and a regular guest performer at festivals and events.

As a mentor for new poets and host of a popular bi-monthly poetry group in Swansea, David is immersed in the literary world of his city.

His use of descriptive, easy to understand language enables the reader/listener to confront often complex issues and ideas which expose human faults and achievements

In the summer of 2016, David's short story collection 'Single Tears' will be on sale.

It Was Nearly Dark

"We didn't have his body to bury or to burn," she said. "There was no need to summon from Hell those men black as ravens or their cars black as murder; no need for chiselled planks or the hidden man's finger that lowers the platform that feeds the furnace. But the men who were there were in stiff white shirts that hid their ink-filled arms but not their wind-tanned faces or greying beards; small men from Asia and giants from colder lands, men from an obvious maritime casting agency. And other men, friends, land-bound, but who would also drown one day, breathless in their oceans of papers and books."

She stood, trembling, but not with cold. She was intent on continuing but was not struck with urgency. She seemed to want the tale to be paused, for drama, for impact. Or perhaps she was just imagining the words. Her eyes were magnified through tears, mirrors of her pain. She held my hand as she continued.

"At the Mission, while the men drank their beer, or swelled their tea with rum from their secret-flasks, there were just the two women; her and I, she who called herself his cousin, a woman I had never heard tell of, a woman of sad smiles and quiet comforting gestures. And with her that child, with his hair of golden curls, his face even paler than his lips and his eyes of sea-cold blue that could have frozen our souls but ended in shedding the only tears of the day, the tears that we others would know later, alone and with just ourselves to humble. "He's tired and cold. He's just a child. I'll take him back now," the cousin said and squeezed my hand as she left.

David Churchill

"Just a child?" What is Just a child? Just a World?
Just an Ocean?"

As she talked we sat on the only rock on the wide beach
and the waves were barely ripples. It was nearly dark. Her
hands were fumbling to fasten her coat against the
suddenly-felt November chill. I helped her, though I also felt
little control over the moment. As I held her close I could
feel her sobs and her thrumming heart even through our
coats. To me this offered solace, but she had loved him as
a lover and I only as a friend. She started to tell her story
again, as if she was trying to divine the sense of it, as if it
was the first time she had told it.

"The man Olaf, his deck-mate, he told me about it. A sea as
calm as silk, he said. There was only the one strap to
tighten, just the one container to secure. And despite Olaf's
warnings, John decided there was no no need for his belt to
be worn, no need for the "umbilicus", as it's called. It was
the freak of the wave, Olaf said, that came from the depths,
un-seeable, un-knowable. And it chose only John to take
and left the others just yards away without even the tinge of
bitter salt and water to taste on their tongues. And they
searched but they never found him, you know. That's why
we had no body……."

She sobbed with a last retching horror but was suddenly
calm. She sought my eyes; her own were enlarged in the
reflection of her tears and in their pools was a new warmth,
an echo of a sudden and mad realisation.

"He's not gone, you know, not forever," she whispered.

"That child at the funeral, the little merman, those blue eyes – he was not the cousin's child. He was *him*, he was *John*, it was John crying to be reborn, looking for the umbilicus to save himself from eternity. He must be reborn, I must give him his life back."

She seem restored, as if her life now had an impelling direction. She still held my eyes in the mirror of hers.

"Will you help me to give him his existence? He would like it to be you. He will live again through us. And he will live again through the love we have for him."

•

At the due time, I sat in the suite as she endured the pain until the final excruciating moments drowned her. And as he cried for the first time, still attached to the line of his life, she and I looked to his eyes to see if they were the brown of hers or the hazel of mine. Or the freezing sea-cold blue we were both terrified of and longing for.

Just a few weeks later I found the note she had left me. It was poetry, I suppose. I knew I would never see her or the child again. I see John sometimes in my mind if I am walking on the beach. On her note, she had written:

"It is only the dead who make the sounds you will know them by; the dead and the sailors who plough the Sea; while the living, with lips wetted by rain and stained by the earth they kiss, and the lovers in their loving, must ache in the silence that ends their days."

Snake Charmer (Part 1)

The look you gave was a viper
That moved with twist and silence.
And the moment was heavy-filled with
The sting of nails in an open-wound;
The happy, lost days now remembered
Only as an objective, bloodless mist
Dissolving as it meets the rise
Of fractured frost and coiling air.
Left is only the sense of pallid unreason,
A play of guilty sex and petty misdemeanour
Taking a stage never dressed for its opening night.
And we persist, unmanned but unbroken,
To seek a salvation slow to reveal
The limits of all we never shared.

Snake Charmer (Part 2)

And the look you gave was a viper
That moved with twist and silence
And spat venom that burned the bones
Of a body still sullied with love,
Carried away and swallowed by jaws dislocated;
And ribs inside, tickle and torment
And friction and pulse, digesting,
For itself only, the morsels of flesh
Sticky and substantial
That makes it sleep,
That makes it deadly.

David Churchill

This White Place

I must not be here now.
The memories are deep with regret
Not rich with the joys and anxieties of
The shared and binding thread.

I cannot face Us or Ours, even in describing the past.
This white place was always yours, the village, the culture
The mad, engulfing, light-filtering family-tree.
And I stocked and stored and never threw away, in order
To hide in the debris a semblance of a single me.

I will move now to a new house and live with an old faith.
I will decorate its nooks, its crannies and fill its tables with
Fresh fruit, and fresh flowers and fresh bread: move
To where the windows will smile with light and not frame
Those dark, high trees on which the shadows hang,
Clothes discarded and thrown by a
Naked scarecrow past.

David Churchill

The Sisters *

So who do you pray to, Sisters? Now your eldest is taken
by Man;
Your Immaculate eldest, ascended from Grace with the
eyes like stones
And the cool, alabaster, pouting disdain.

Stand for now in your cloud of marble, silver and white
With your hands in front, unformed, gloveless, so no
Devil can lurk behind, nor sin conceal in your Vanity.
And stand for now in pose and precedence, unsmiling,
Saddened, untouched, with the glow of cube and bee-hive,
Chiffon windows of holy, shimmering island light.

Stand now for your Sister.

And yet your tulip-stem necks and your surreal, viola faces
Are portraits of not just eternal innocence.
In your eyes, too, the dream of Wedding's Eve, in your eyes
The shock of light, the herald Dawn, the Fateful Day,
The single moment when the flesh will replace with
Substance your aura of imponderable time.

Age-Old Story

And finally, Methuselah thought:
"Right, that's it for me.
I've put up with enough bad weather to last me
A lifetime without having to go through all that
Chopping down trees, all that hammering and nailing,
All that rounding up of His creatures."
And in years I have reached nine-six-nine
A neat, somehow Biblical number so easily divided
By the happy Holy Trinity.
And I have left them, my son and his sons,
With names so ludicrous that
They are sure to be never forgotten.

And imagine the fuss and arguments when the Waters
Finally come and their Ark floats miraculously away.
It was bad enough last Passover when all those sons
And wives and their sons and wives
Couldn't even agree on the colour of the table-cloths
To spread to hold all His sacred bounties.
And Heavens help us later, when those birds return
With branch in beak or fish in claw:
What will He do to console his scolded children,
Dampened with regret and wrinkled with resent?
There'll be a show like never before, called Rainbow
The World's Wonder , when beheld in the valley below.

So old you may be, Sir, but do not covet my name,
The name that means "Death Shall Bring Judgment"
So old you may be but never as old as Old Methuselah.
Live long but live in the hope that God never grants you the
Same Gracious curse that makes you too live eternally.

The Happiness Of Ignorance

My own words were difficult to hear;
The chasm of confusion unbridgeable,
The low rumbling and higher sing-song
Filling any space for pause or reflection,
And yet creating an indefinable comfort,
The melody staccato, beating the cracked rhythm
Of love and happiness nurtured through ignorance.
To learn there was song or chanting,
To learn there was kneeling and cushions
And repeated mantras and silly rhymes,
Drowning out the boom of anxieties
Of a world before the birth of drop-out panacea
Or floating strata-forms of Nirvana clouds.
We sang as a chorus, no practised harmony,
Bass and treble and alto divided only by accident
Of throat untutored and unplaced in scale.

My older brother had blue, my other brother brown,
And my own were still undetermined between
The speckle of green and hazel.

Is this then the all of what I remember:
The singing and rainbows of their eyes?
So ask me again, my son, when the world has turned again.
Ask me again, and perhaps the tune will then be sung
With a voice now broken and unable
Despite the years to catch the meaningful phrases.

Muscular Christianity

The man never waited to catch the single feeling
Of his son passing into the night, cold as the iron wrought
To surround the field of mud, caking hard the heart
For the greater morass yet to come.
And masters with their mutton-chops, pedalling their
Raleighs and peddling their lies:

Here's to the Puppet Empire, dancing by the thread of
cotton traded for slaves, spun by the women
Too broken now for anything but the work-house gates.
All in the name of a Natural cause, all for those selected
To carry the Burden, those who ruled where
Even God chose not to look.

Down the years you can sense the folly,
You can taste the gall on your flabby upper lip.
But watch your screen
And see the old men justify, just once more,
A new War in the East that needs fighting.
Fail again to catch the children and
Fail again to catch the breath,
As we re-new and compound our
Inglorious, our vainglorious past.

Future On your Tongue

You sat with the future on your tongue,
Avoiding the gaze that focussed on your crisis.
And I sat in curious disinterest, almost hoping
To save you from the channel of suffering,
The gross negligence offered to your authority.
Then, in reassertion, you recited your script
And, re-asserted. fought to master an almost-smile.
And the flood of our righteous objection passed
Unacknowledged, except to re-direct to
a higher, more exalted Deity of dispute.
And Pontius, you rubbed your delicate palms
And you laced your delicate fingers,
And grey shining white and duty done,
You moved away and thrust yourself with daggers
To see if your blood would still run crimson and
The stain soak your immaculate, white-washed hands.

Sarah Evans

Sarah was born in Cheshire and grew up in the Peak District of Derbyshire. As an adult, she returned to her family roots in Wales. She now lives in Swansea and is an active participant in poetry events within the city.

Sarah draws on life experiences and self healing to craft her poetry   Her use of current street talk and carefully chosen words enriches her work and places her poetry within easy reach of all ages.

Sarah has a wide range of poetic influences which include Swansea born poet, Dylan Thomas

Lost at Sea

In my mind I see wave after wave,
Timorous, thunderous on sand.
The sea is my mind, a torment,
A ceaseless ferment.
Dragged under to discover terrible treasures.
Fish and ship bones.
Prehistoric phantoms with jewelled fangs,
Lanterns guttering behind the cages of their eyes.
Ghosts of decayed emotions
Spewing out past lives like jellyfish tails
I can never live in the present.
Leaving, arriving, giving, taking.
I'm a shark, I bite savage.
I cannot forgive the sea
It's salt in the quick of our tenderness.
The creative fluid between us phosphorescent with desire.
I am descending in my submarine
To plumb the unconscious depths
Are you receiving me beloved? Over.
The lifeboat went out to my mayday call.
The crew were daunted
Bodies poured out of the ship
Boys in twenty foot waves
The white horses stampeded the hull,
Tossed from crest to crest
Spume sprayed spine
The lifeboat turned back
My love is now a shipwreck and I a landlubber

Sarah Evans

Paranoia

Knives out for the pocket fishwives
Muses of smilopaths and serial poets.
Drinking gallons of lines down
Does the stomach settle for it
Or will it regurgitate it like a computer
Randomly composing fluorescent
Compassionate hemorrhoids

Attack on a poet

Quick, quick, emergency call an ambulance.
There's been a poetry attack.
Love bomb, sent straight to slay me.
Shellshock reverberates around the room.
The poet's made the audience faint with
One-liner bullets from his heart.
Cocktails for two spilt upon the floor,
The ice is broken.
He's a wanted man,
One man who dunnit!
Will anybody slap him on the back and buy him a drink
But no, he is a slut-smith touting awares.
He has melted us all and we are oozing
Out of the door without paying, Emotion in motion.
Not even in appreciation
Stun-gunned into inarticulacy.
Uttering stutteringly his gut monkey wrench poems.
Beauty of his beast.
We will have to live our lives differently now we have
heard.
"NOW GO OR WE WILL SET THE DOGS ON YOU"

Apart

I live on dreams and screams
And wear tattered garments of happiness,
The wind blows me "around the world
In eighty days".
I try to put it into words
But it comes out silent,
Like mouthing frozen smoke rings
That crash into tinkling glass
So pretty and so cold.
I see your story,
I, "the fool on the hill".
And though it moves me,
I am perfectly still.
Who jumbled up the pieces of our lives
Just to see where they would land?
With creative divinity, we understand.

Elegy

Where all the golden eggs are laid,
Where all the promises are made,
Where all the princesses are saved,
Flowers crowned,
Fountains spray.
Baby beings of light and angel trees
Are decked with falling trails of leaves.
There came night upon his milky steed,
To sweep the world away,
To heaven, squeezing through the pearly gates.
God's tears give us benefit of doubt,
Where they fall and cry,
Like arrows of angels, to our hearts they fly.

Sarah Evans

Spider love

Spider dances, her body quivering with venom.
A tangled web with which to deceive,
Rainbows drown her home,
Brooks running into blood turn to frozen crystal with
her icy breath.
She blocks the plug hole so her babies can't escape.
Marching left right, left right nazi saluting, up and
over the sleepers binding them closer and closer with
a golden thread yellow ribbons of sunlight entwined to
make glowing capsules of light.

Light as a feather they bob downstream, flotsam
and jetsam for the tourists who don't look too closely,
The spider sings and weaves faster and faster 'til
she burns up into silver stardust and the ghosts split
into atoms.
The children learn about this in school,
Quantum physics for beginners which fly off the page
into their hearts bursting like supernovas.

Sarah Evans

Suicide

This person's dead,
That person's dead,
Wear your purple heart on your sleeve
Thee I do not mean to peeve.
Love lies bleeding in a thousand tales
Sorrow in me oh heavenly one.
We are sailing into the night
Off the edge of the world
Love upon the burning deck.
Slow stars hammer my brain
Following the waves' refrain,
Break, break me like a stone
We are cells that divide and grow again.

Sensitive

Ants on top of a mountain
petrified limbs in silhouetted lightening freeze
the volcanic ash settles and stretches in a minutiae,
millennium
to be the rock of ages.
lichen phosphorescence lit by its reflex patterns
shifts shape to sidestep from a smitten meteorite's kiss,
near miss
rocks back in its seat
and whispers to itself
he loves me, he loves me not
at the lip of the moon's sad sigh
the tide pours in
the planets recoil
and she's gone again
light years away.

Sarah Evans

Mum and Dad

Some part of me is growing
And I love you always, my darling.
The memories of your cherishing, crowd in,
Your bloody mindedness and the rounded
Part doth please me.
Give me back your life so I can play it back on video.
Catch your dreams alight unto the sky.
Watch them drop like sparks in grace
As you lie sleeping under the hill
Riding with King Arthur's knights
In your innocence 'til you meet dad
And are whole.
There the heavens unfold in glory
And hope is saved.

Golden Shot

Oh god of mice and mice and men,
'You're in the Army' now,
Alone, fighting on a star,
Trying to reach the moon with a teaspoon.
Meteorites flashing past the window,
Flying pigs to make you cry,
Sat nav. guided by the scent of flowers.
Homeward bound to projectile planned
Bigger and beyond,
The Buddha whispering in your ear.

Out there

There's only so much green you can absorb by
Osmosis, after that you start to become an alien and
Start to photosynthesise.
Travelling from beauty spot to beauty spot, strung
Together, punctuated by traffic lights
Modern graffiti graphics emblazoned with aerosol can
Spray across the sky.
Elizabethan black spots, heart shaped
And cupid lipped, foppery, bewigged, powdered
With bird nests, cuckoo, cuckoo.
Sometimes when you call, hearing your echo
I feel so happy......
The sound of one hand clapping?
The secret code of a woodpecker's tap.
Meanwhile in another part of the forest
Comes the answer.

Sarah Evans

The Velvet Poet

He wears a hair shirt and hash aftershave.
By day he sports a loose Superman onesie
And carries a plastic suitcase
From which he feeds the pigeons in the park.

He reads from crumpled sheets
And stained cuffs,
Lives on smoothies and fags,
Rolls his own sushi.
A connoisseur of café coffees
But banned from the new Kardomah.
Careless with swear words,
Flicking them across Swansea Bay
To sink like mines.
Knows the price of a round,
The value of beauty in his head,
Purple prose with ink of crushed rose,
Has friends in low places
In case of emergencies.
Bites off heads of bats and hecklers.
Is he happy?, who knows but he thinks
Therefore he exists.

Sarah Evans

All Roads lead to Rome

A bell on every tooth, in truth,
The peculiar wizard concocting his lizard spells
With hobo spiders and pickled bits.
Sparks from his fire, fairy-dust saltpeter,
On his shoulders, a cape of dandruff silver frost.
He looks through his widespread fingers
To see the wide world and pulls out a spotted handkerchief
With paperclips and old cocktail sausages still on sticks.
He spins the ocean into whirls
So they dump their mermaids on shore,
leave them gasping for a sailor to kiss them quick
And they become bowsprits.
Up and over the waves in wetsuit and flippers,
His mask a diving bell to avoid the purply bends.
He works his magic live and dangerous.
Some with love,
Some with fate,
Some with kingdoms,
Some with service.
Light to dark,
The reason for his treason
Is the sprinkling of an eye,
We laugh and then we cry.

Teifion comes from the east side of Swansea, an area with a strong industrial past.

As a performing poet, he draws upon humour and memories which reflect upon people from the area. His work includes a vernacular dialect that is fast disappearing from the region.

He writes about the natural environment that surrounded him as a child: rivers, woods, ponds, quarries and cliffs. He has an interest in politics and although it is included in his work, the subject does not dominate it.

Teifion's first published book, 'Licking slugs, riding cows' is available from the author.

Not a Ripple, Save for the Trail of a Swan.

If ever I was blessed 'twas then: a mile from Ambleside.
The last crumbs of August brewed crispy leaves
that dripped around you both, as you hopped in
dungarees, quick as squirrels. You sang a song of
sixpence, and your words were floating bubbles that I
followed to the highest point above the wooden house.

If ever there was sun-blazed orange it was then.
All drowsy now my strolling eyes. And down below,
'tween us and Grasmere, the day had made a lake.
A small lake: a pond, compared to Windermere,
or Buttermere, or Coniston, or Crummock.
How small you both were; and how calm the water:
not a ripple, save for the trail of a swan.
And my heart sprang, and was on its bike.

If ever I have wished for wings, 'twas then.
We'd have skimmed the lake, dipping for fish.
We'd have swished and picked; wrapped our feet
round every branch, their knots and curls. We'd have
dropped on every weathered fence-post; praised loud
the rub of moss, the smell of rotting logs.

If ever an evening fluttered and sang it was then.
You waved your sticks at all the oaks in Thistle Wood,
and Crow Wood, and Nab Wood. You cart-wheeled,
loopy on your hands, my pretty maids: ruffling ferns,
and the dimming day. The world was from here to
Rydal Fell; and left to me, I'd have pickled us in a genie's
jar, kept you far from cynics, weavers and frauds;
from jack the lads, sonny jims, and blue-eyed boys.
If ever I was broken it was then: a mile from Ambleside.

I watched you skip and sway: your sticks flicking
acorns, as we traipsed back, down the path that crept
towards our forest plot: towards an ending and a beginning.
Rattled now, I caught the sound of drumbeats.
The week had passed: I cursed its speed. I knew
I'd swopped a summit for a road of holes.

Was Next I Held a Thought

You there, unleashed in schoolyard soup.
As usual you'd greased your wings, propelled
on miracle air. You spun slapdash with your
electric friends. From the gate I watched you
spill into your room draped with painted leaves;
your presence ticked by Miss Pilinszky. I wished
on you a walled in world: north to paint your leaves,
south for scooping frogspawn, east to find
a wattle fort, west for planting seeds.

Strolling back. I passed, as I do most mornings,
the woman with the string belt walking her dog;
the rotting caravan that smells of stuff
spread wet on fields; Mog's exploding garden
with its jungle of sprouts; the man with the
iffy hat who thinks he's William Tell; and Dai the Bird's
monotonous pigeons.

Fixed upon nothing, I came to where the milk churns
once stood, way back; and me short-arsed, scabby kneed.

Was next I held a thought! It trickled first, then grew:
sour, brown, with prongs. An imp with knotted lips,
I lobbed it sharp on Mog's compost. Rigid though,

it tracked my heels, clung to the toe of my boot.
It stroked its chin, eyed me up and down, then leapt
back inside my half-cocked head.

It arched its back, flared its nostrils. Cold, harsh:
it spoke of you, my grandchild, now measuring for Miss
the length of paper snakes. Uselessly I smoothed
its goblin head. It babbled on, of hard blows to come:
knaves and fixers with new brews of illusion.

The thought had spied my brittle shield; it bulldozed on:
a poxy nuisance, devil's bell in every tooth.

In fear, I gripped its throat, sliced its tongue. I dragged it
three fields, tracks of ice, a hemlock wood .I thumped
its tackle, kicked its groin. I smothered it with other
thoughts: a porridge of sighs soft voiced.

And I wished for it a mind's corner; no-man's-land;
Mog's rotting heap. But oiled by stealth,
this single thought had gathered sway and held
its thread with you, and you, and you; and painted leaves.

Shall I Give You a Right Old Eyeful?

Shall I give you a right old eyeful? Shall I? Shall I
tell you of someone who bothers the world? Who
knows about money. He does not farm, he does
not build, he does not make things, fix a broken pipe,
heal the sick, dig a well, run machines, or drive a bus.
There, he squats there. Watch him! He knows all
about money: every minute, every hour of the day.
He knows how it sleeps and the time it rises, the time

Teifion Hughes

it cleans its teeth, picks its nose, wipes its arse, combs
its hair. He knows what it wants for breakfast, dinner
and tea, and what it eats and drinks on special occasions.
He knows when to take it for a walk, scrub its back,
pat its head, tickle its chin; and the precise time
to check its pulse. He knows its rosy days, its fickle days;
when it wants to get its leg over, and when it wants
to give birth. He knows when it's restless and looks to
book a flight; when it wants to pull a fast one, and where
it likes to lie low. He knows the shift of its every shadow,
the sum of all its dreams. He knows its bug bears and the
speed with which it turns to show its claws. He knows of its
rare gestures, as he leans back to gob on a world of cuts.
To be sure there's music in his head: a kind
of triumphal march. In his castle he is king.
Left to me: I'd sling his hard drive in the moat.

A Revolving Door

The goggle-box. Dead immigrants, their world shrunk to the
back of a truck; a robot in a suit says something old. Vets
help an alpaca in distress. There's a baking competition:
Brenda hopes her bara-brith will do the trick. Customs
officers: there's a man with a suitcase full of squid. Tourists
make love, drunk on a Greek resort: they get sand up their
rear ends. Dog's dinner surgery: a woman weeps through
bandage.
*My eyes shift. Through my window there's a shrub, and on
it the patience of a spider. She fixes the dregs of her
battered web. Across the road, the sycamores. Magpies are
yapping.*
Dysentery. Children die drinking swill: a call goes out for
wells, with a number for a whip-round.

A man's behind the wheel of a new Ferrari F12. Five year old daughters, high heeled on a stage, their grinning faces daubed. Most haunted homes: the team visit Hellhound Hall. Cowboys take a year to build a porch. Tourists make love, drunk on a Spanish resort: they get sand up their rear ends. Back to back episodes of Britain's hardest lifers.
I look outside. Head down, she spins: her web's half done. The trees will soon be stripped by winter. I'll glimpse between them frosty hills and Tank Farm Road. Jackdaws chase a squirrel.
Sicily. Dead immigrants, their world shrunk to the hull of a ship; a robot in a suit says something old. A couple look for a fantasy house by the sea, with one a yacht's thrown in; this they take a shine to. People pelt round shops, grabbing tubs and tins.
Serial hoarders: in goes Mary, the smell knocks her back a bit. Tourists make love, drunk on a Turkish resort: they get sand up their rear ends. Much is made of the 'new nazi season that kicks off soon on channel five.'
I turn away. Her knitting's done. In the morning her silk will sway stuffed with dewdrops. Woodpeckers drum their galleon masts. And I too, claim my patch: I wield my snout with all wild things.
Women with sticks sift through a dump: babies, strapped to their backs, are surrounded by flies. Police chase car thieves through Bristol. There's a new record for the number of people on the back of a jeep. Chefs make the world's largest outdoor pizza. Tourists, sex, drunk, resort. And rest assured, there's sand up their rear ends. A kind of clay and clumps of ice are found on Mars. A man hugs a crocodile. *Outside, Jays climb the sycamores. I praise the spider's tapestry. And I think about the bravery of immigrants, the cost of a well; an infant with a tin of filth. I curse the oldness of a robot in a suit.*

Teifion Hughes
Salmon Run

This morning he was nine years old. The ocean knew
and offered him songs, breakfast in bed. He downed his
krill, his pilchards. He's to shift from Greenland to Welsh
stream, his nook of birth. Four foot, a sixty pounder: he
travels east.

Wagging, fathoms under froth, he'll rough it for a
thousand miles towards Worm's Head:
Blow Hole to the left, Devil's Bridge, Low Neck. Leaning
right, a mile from Fall Bay, passing Crabart, Tear's Point,
Paviland, Blackhole Gut.
He's steered by smell: of sunken chains, of crusted hulls;
of all that seeps through the skin of a hill, from the
shape of a bay. Past Culver Hole, the clamour of gulls
dipping to a digger's fork, the tub of lug; past Seven Slades,
Mitchin Hole; and Bacon Hole, where a boy flew a
crimson kite.

From Pwlldu to Snaple Point, sniffing barrels and a
smuggler's rib.
At Rothers Sker he said farewell to friends bound for
streams at Merthyr.
Shorelines north he swam, through the pores of a dock
mud town,
remembering the river's scent that still whispered coal,
copper, limestone.

By Clydach Bridge he'd grown a hump, curved jaws; at fall
and rapid, silver scales had coloured red. Head down
through Trebanos, past the Gwachel * and the furtive rod of

Hywel Price, who stood, sly as herons, with his bailiff
dodging squint, and his alphabet of flies.

Out to nab a salmon too was Joe the Goat from Glais.
But this poem's fish leapt ten foot beyond the net, then
kicked for Ynysmeudwy. And between the stones of
Craig-y-Nos and Lyn-y-Fan-Fawr he lay among the
minerals of Brecon. A streambed felt his flat splash, the
place that once baptised him.

At boiling point, father to a ruck of orange eggs; by
midnight he was dead: a champion, magnetised by
autumn's latch.

He floated, belly to the moon. And me, noble fish: I envy
your rounded life.
Trap upon trap; crag on crag; each narrow gap: how you
rose.
Just the sweep of it; be praised: from Greenland to Welsh
gravel!

Spirit of the Same Breath

I'm thoughts of things that happen together,
I'm spirits of the same breath.
I am many times upon the same time,
I am many tongues upon the same tongue.
A scrounger of maps,
I have wings enough
to pour my eyes into your eyes.

I can show you many things:

Teifion Hughes

I will show you a boy
who walks along a troubled ridge.
The boy stops. He turns.
He's lobbing stones at riflemen.
A snake-charmer curves one hand,
as a desert flower is cooled by a breeze
whose sister rubs a scarecrow's chin.

I will show you a girl knocking out rugs:
her head is sighing with dreams.
She sleeps, she weaves, she sleeps,
she weaves. She sleeps.
A shipwreck sways in scattered fathoms
as a heart is carved on the bark of a tree
whose brother feeds a forest mouth.
I'll show you a poet doubting her worth.
She measures her words: she meddles.
Beneath the soil an earthworm swigs
a weeping rib and thinks it's Christmas,
as a raven climbs: the only thing that budges
on a hundred hills of snow.

I'll show you someone blown to bits,
who's come to know the happiness upon a face
is there for someone else.
Now see someone licking lips,
who'll gulp enough to choke a donkey:
chucks what's left. A child is drinking filth.

The moment thaws. Time passes,
and I shift to a new breath,
wetting the appetite with new messages.
Pouring my eyes into your eyes.

Even Horse-flies

All he wanted of the world was its wildness.
The rest he let slip silently free, drifting further, further back.

A half world, he'd always thought: its counting houses,
its counting house kings.
Its tax pathways carved by stealth, how silent the stealth-
men.
Its furnaces, its drumbeats and bugles.
Its clipped wings; its old ground; its cold mouth.

And so, he drew his map, and marked the measure of
nearby things.

Starlings strung on pylons over Talycopa fields,
all mumbling their love of tractors and Leyshon's corn.
A belted hedge of hips and haws, slow slopes down
Gobfull Road*. The shiggling stick his grandson wagged
made weasels bolt. Or were they stoats?

He said good morning to the crows: his boots on Jackdaw
Tips.
By Crymlyn Farm's hard muck, where lobworms traced his
winter dance, he ate the wind that chucked up rooks.
But he worshipped most the carrion's caw
through black frosted oaks above the Nant.

Railway banks by Ket* and Tap* and Ebenezer:
bracken adder tracking voles, its V with zigzag black.
Quarry ponds, where midnight mammoths drank:
the swim of grass snakes, four foot, munching frogs.
The Pentre, where corrugated sheets shrouded warm
the slow-worms.

Teifion Hughes

He walked hard the dram road to Carreg Bica*:
Drummau's perch with mossy poles.
Then, knee-deep the autumn hay: he swished its crop
of summer fossils.

Among the scrub and hooves: green glides and quivers,
how green the grasshopper, its twenty second chirp on
Summer Hill.
In a wall's gap: bold cuckoo bees, a cracking find.
And just across the cwm* between sycamores that creaked:
the moon's polar glow.

All in all, a narrow stretch. He praised it: from its hiding pike
to the snail that chewed his beans; to the earwig's apple
feast;
to a millipede's whirl, its ninety legs; to the woodlouse
(cousin of crab and lobster); to moths, big as doughboys,
nudging glow.

And though they puffed his hands, he'd go out to meet
the horse-flies as far as Heifers' Bridge.

Rebecca is a freelance features writer, editor and poet.

Her poetry has been featured on Radio 4's Poetry Workshop and has appeared in anthologies including Bristol Poetry Can, Red Poets and Blackheath Countercultural Review.

She is a regular performing poet at festivals and spoken word events and has run a series of children's poetry workshops.

One of Rebecca's stranger experiences was having one of her haiku turned into sushi wrapping for an art installation in London.

Rebecca's published chap book, 'Music of the Sea' is available from the author.
www.writerscafe.org/BeckyLowe

Rebecca Lowe

Dylan

He always had an inkling for the sea,
That moon-drift child with the seaweed curls,
His laughter melted sea foam,
Scooping up in shovels, the dwindling dregs
Patted into proud battlements,
Watched as the water slowly inundated
Crumbling moats and crooked towers,
To sink beneath the ever-growing storm.

His first kisses were at this quayside,
Soft, like wet sand, he took her
Mermaid hand in his; she shrank back,
Eyes wide as a seal's, afraid of
The coming tide. They lobbed pebbles
Ferociously at waiting rocks, placed
Seashells to their ears, listened
To hear the flowing voices
Of Sirens, in the tide's
Ebb and fall.

And, in his later years,
Landlocked, would peer
Into the lulling froth of beer
And imagine mermaids
Pulling him back in again
To the dark and creamy depths...

....Caught out by Rhossili* tides
They awaken from the belly of the Worm*
To a Wonderland of giant bluebells,
Reflected across the gaping yawn of the bay
To distant shores and bobbing pygmy boats,

And feel themselves explorers
In a strange, exotic land...

Somewhere in a dim hotel,
He's a rocking boat,
All adrift;
She flashes him a fish-hook smile,
Reels him in, gills flapping,
But at his embrace, dissolves
Into bubbles,
Her laughter reverberating
Across the waters.

Cogs

You are cogs, cutting me
With the sharp teeth
Of your logic.
And I bite back,
Turn your words
Over and over,
Each rotation of the blade,
Becomes more raw,
Cuts deeper,
Reopening old wounds
Into fresh ribbons
Of blood.
Each time we re-crank
This tired machine,
We resort to the same
Mechanical motions,
Perfectly syncopated,
Become automata.

Rebecca Lowe

Morning After

The morning is screaming herself awake
Through chinks of glass and tired curtains,
Refusing to let sleep the hungover remains
Of last night's dregs and strays,

Spittle-tongued and spin-headed
Past drowsing streetlamps,
Tumbling heels still slick
With last night's rain,
Pick their way through
Pavings, past barbed-wire,
Padlocked doors
Splinter sharp

And looking on
Like disapproving aunts,
The cold and clammy clouds
As stark and stone-cold sober,
Silent as a tripwire.

Rebecca Lowe

Portrait of the Artist

Against his better judgment,
He ushers her in to the secret place,
Slips the latch, and there she stands,
Incongruous in her femininity, here,
Where everything is masculine,
Leather sofas smell of pipe smoke,
Gentleman's cologne and the
Faintest whiff of horse sweat,
Here, she sets up her easel
And begins to paint...

Gently at first, with softest
Brushstrokes, she takes in the
Contours of his neck, the slope
Of his thighs, with her eyes,
Strips him of skin, blood, and bone,
And feels him move beneath the
Cool sweep of her gaze, feels him
Come alive in the swirl of colour –
Burnt sienna, vermilion,
Rouge, white.

As she paints, they talk a little,
Nothing special; he comments on
The weather; she nods her head,
Notices how his tongue plays at his teeth
As he talks, how his eyelids flutter like
Moths when nervous, the gossamer hairs
That lie upon the nape of his neck
Like a baby's, captures the slightly lopsided
twitch at the corner
Of his mouth when he starts to smile.

Rebecca Lowe

For his part, he shuffles uneasily in his
Sunday Best clothes, and wishes it were done,
Aware of something significant passing
That he can't quite place a finger on,
but knows it's gone.

At the finish, they stare together at
The canvas, like two newly-acquainted,
Agree that it is, indeed, a very
Good likeness, that she has exactly caught
The essence of him. And afterwards he will
Pay handsomely, take the canvas away,
Satisfied, to hang upon the wall of
Some stately home or other,
Where he will come to rest,
Stiff, and unmoveable.

And if they do not meet again,
Do not pass comment,
Never touch at all,
It scarcely matters.

She knows she had him captured once,
Once held him.

Blood and Water

'Mummy' –
They say the word
Like it's a title I'm supposed to own,
But I don't, not yet,
Any more than I feel I own
This precious bundle in my arms,
Who looks at me with the same mixture
Of amazement and bewilderment
I feel myself.

And so, I start to give in,
Day by day, surrendering more of myself
To your tiny will,
Willing slave,
Feeding and changing
And changing and feeding
In an endless, sleepless wave,
Until days become nights,
Nights become days,
As if, through practice,
I will make myself expert,
As if through familiarity,
I will make of us family.

Though my fingers fumble
At each unfamiliar button,
I fear to pick you up
Lest you should slip
Through my arms like butter,
And sleep so close to your cot
I can hear each rumble, each snuffle,
And place you determinedly on your back,

Rebecca Lowe

Your little arms outspread
Like a swimmer,
Who has left me marooned
On a shore where nothing fits,
Whale-like, I am out of my element,
Beached, I cry,
Somewhere, submerged
Between waves of love
And fear, the salt pricks,
I am ocean bound.

Precious one, you lie
Like a butterfly drying your wings,
Not yet ready to fly;
Tentatively, I pick you up,
Feel you mould your body
To my holding,
Feel the love that is stronger
Than blood and water,
Feel you slowly becoming
Daughter.

First Kicks

Not a kick at first
But a beating of wings,
A heart's flutter,
Not a shouting into being
But a murmur, a whisper
Of assent.

On the screen
She is grainy, grey,
Her fingers translucent,
Clasped, in prayer,
Her pixelated face
Stares back through
Layers of time,
Suspended.

Her skin, a spider-skein
Of threads, still weaving
To vein, corpuscle,
Tender fontanelle –

We gaze across
An ocean's distance,
Farther than we
Have ever travelled,
Closer than we
Will ever be again

Rebecca Lowe

Conviction

Narrowing his eyes, the Judge said: 'How do you plead?'
'We plead with the evidence of our own lives,
Which have never grown weary of defending the innocent
From the weapons of power; though in your eyes,
we may be guilty
Let our actions now be placed on trial;
We stand by our convictions.'

Bridling, the Judge stood fast: "It's not for me to judge
The rights or wrong of war; Enter your plea:
Guilty or Not Guilty? You must understand, what's on trial
Here is how your actions impacted on the lives
Of others - decent men, proper men, made to feel guilty
For the legal selling of arms to protect the innocent.'

And now you show that you, too, are not so innocent,
You who sit upon the thrones of power and judgement,
Who fill us with the flames of Holy terror, guilt-trip
Us into believing in our utter depravity, so that we plead
Wholeheartedly for a Redeemer to enter our lives,
A fire we cannot quench, no matter how hard we try.

Listen… I know it is difficult to do, but try, really try,
Try to imagine that we were each born innocent,
That inside each of us, no matter how imperfect, lives
The potential for love. I say it again:
Try hard not to judge,
But imagine, in each of us, the capacity to plead
The innate beauty of Another, to find ourselves not guilty.

Rebecca Lowe

But we are none of us wholly immune.
All bear the guilt
Of collective centuries of war and hatred, trying
To resolve our differences through military might;
our one plea
To be spared the obscenity of watching the innocent die
 So they must die unnoticed, safe from the judgment of
The world's media, must not intrude upon our private lives.

And so the men in suits must continue to make their living,
Must not see the lacerated limbs of children, lest they
feel a pang of guilt,
Must not enlist conscience lest they lose their proper
sense of judgment,
I ask, with all respect: Is it they or us who should be
standing trial?
Which of us is guilty, and which innocent?
You ask, 'Your Worship' (In Whose Worship?), you ask….
how do we plead?

We have but one plea, which is to spare the lives
Of the innocent, and put the guilty
On trial.
May God be our Judge.

Mark Lyndon

Mark was born in the heart of the Gower Peninsula
and is a performing poet.

His work is inspired by the natural and coastal
environments of the area and reflects their colours
and hues.
The personification of places and things shapes his
poetry and allows the reader/listener to get to know the
personality of the environment he sees.

Mark's heartfelt homage to the superlative Welsh coastline
"Once more unto the beach, dear friends, once more'
is still available for purchase from the author.

Poetic Justice

A fusty, feisty judge craned forward, sneering
contemptuously at parlous defendants hunched
obsequiously in the dock.
He was a piteous, pitiless paradox of a man,
fantastically physically frail, yet ostensibly omnipotent.
That twig-like big-wig was a tediously fastidious
grammarian. Hubris was his sibilant essence.
Hoity-toity Lord Verbosity was pomposity personified.
Half-cut, he harrumphed and bellowed a pernicious
paragraph of balderdash from his thesaurus.
"You verminous, crass dross, hoi polloi hobbledehoys
stand accused of an unpardonable crime…
.....that of using a double negative in a sentence!
What an unfathomable gaffe; what unutterable guff!
A capital offence!
Infra dig!"
"But we never done nothing, M'lud," opined the belittled
illiterate.
"Quite," quipped this smug sot, whippet-quick, peremptorily
quaffing a tot.
Our despicable despot was arrantly arrogant, abhorrently
aberrant, apparently errant and idiotically grammatically
idiosyncratic.
Being unusually delusional, he believed himself to legally
be an antecedent of a split infinitive and the definite article.
Even as a child, he played pass the past participle, while
solecisms were anathema like asthma to him.
Mum and dad were palindromes but he called them
brackets because he thought they were his parentheses.
He actually was a pronoun.
One once saw him serve a conjunction with an
injunction but without compunction.

Mark Lyndon

He deemed the letter I to be dotty and feared T so didn't cross it.

This puffed-up pipsqueak considered contractions an infraction and, slurring absurdly, averred that he heard the silence of dropped aitches.

Seeing double during a singularly purple patch of posey prose, the colourful arbiter of justice purportedly turned plural.

He was not slow to cut a précis to the quick.

That cadaverous caricature loved the often-hyphenated, all-consuming allure of tongue-twisting, linguistic gymnastics and forever endeavoured to be clever by presuming to put prepositions in appropriate places and pop onomatopoeia when it appeared.

He seemed impossibly possessive about his apostrophes and was even odd about an oxymoron.

Implausibly, the octogenarian contrarian adored and abhorred antonyms, whilst synonyms he saw as right and proper.

Our staid buffer would just stare right through some homophones, for very few won him over.

He vanquished analogies, banished slang, languished in anguish about language, could not be doing with verbs, called nouns names and was fazed by phrases.

The antediluvian man gobbled fruity adages with much voracity but garbled mush without veracity, a plump plum permanently ensconced in his mouth.

Though a number of pithy figures of speech did give him the palindromic pip, he always swore, he never swore.

That fêted fiend was a fiery friend of the circumspect circumflex and admired sonorous assonance as much as similes.

Fictitious sagas made him fractious and, though he ironically thought a plot was a novel idea, clichés he acutely hated.

Malice in Wonderland was his paraphrased nom de plume. Wholly off his iffy head, he royally guttled elaborate vocabulary from nutritious dictionaries at a fun-to-see, fantasy tea party, where incongruous spoonerisms were mad as a hatter, of course.

The floundering judge was found to founder as he faint-heartedly feigned affection for font but was fated to affect a fondness for few forms of feint.

Such was his excruciating infatuation with punctuation that the scoffing boffin bit off more syntax than he eschewed.

Consequently, he was constantly constipated by consonants: disembowelled by vowels, plagued by problems with the colon.

Ominously, commas commonly caused him to pause, comatose.

This iniquitous malcontent looked conspicuously malicious as he lurked adverbially, behind a subordinate, sharpening his clause.

As a venomous serpent, he slithered hither-thither, hissed his dissent, criticised colloquialisms and disrespected dialect, amid an abusive, alliterative avalanche.

With his heinous plethora of precious pretentions and superciliousness strewn in ubiquitous abundance, few perceived that this supposedly perspicacious person was duplicitous and dichotomous.

However, hypocrisy hid behind his high-brow mask.

Here strutted a wide boy wannabe, a closet Cockney geezer, barrelling and bobbling down Bow back-streets, bantering with barrow boys, using the most spectacular vernacular he could muster.

Who would have guessed this poesy obsessive

possessed a repressed desire to talk non-stop, in a bottled-up, over the top glottal stop?

This clandestine predilection for calamitous, slap-dash diction was an addiction.

None knew of his denunciation of enunciation or his renunciation of Received Pronunciation.

Now, visibly discombobulated by an adjectival assault of wintry frostiness, the accursed accused sought a sabbatical from this smatter of matters anagrammatical.

Disingenuous Mister Pot had had enough of the Kettles' hot air and ostentatiously reverted to his high-falutin parlance to blacken their name with his polemic, pluperfect verdict.

It was curtains for certain as that stone-casting word play reached its benighted denouement.

Disparagement swarmed through every pejorative syllable as the befuddled misanthrope chiselled away any lingering pretence at clemency.

"You pleading innocents are guilty of the dastardly offence of incoherence, leading to the precipitous decline of pretty, petty pedantry.

This is contemptible not commendable, yet risibly, you oinking oiks still seem more complacent than complaisant!" he hee-hawed.

"Henceforth, you are to be incarcerated for an eternal spell!" he yelled, rapidly and rabidly, by way of a blatantly belated explanation of the exclamation mark.

Even as he sent them down, he sent them up.

"Can you misbegotten nonentities even spell, spell?" he queried rhetorically, 'twixt awful guffaws.

Wordlessly viewing their endless sentence through the prism of prison bars, misery was the lot of the few.

Mark Lyndon

Malign Reign

Eerie feelings flood o'er our downed town then drown
damned denizens under impending gloom.
Hill-high hove hellish heavens.
Effulgent lightning is nigh, darkening encroaching night's
ominous ambience.
Zigzag sparks of spectacular fury appear, hurled as
animated animus across the purgatorial pall.
Such a luminous streak seems numinous yet heinous.
Hurtling apace, from surrealistically-coloured clouds, an
imaginary dragon's jagged, dagger breaths clout deluged
ground to daze the day's funereal finale with transient
incandescence.
His most monstrous partner in grime lurks and lives livid
inside protean cumulonimbus.
Cacophonous mist is this obstreperous colossus.
Irascibility grows within invisibility, as the thunderous
protagonist makes mayhem happen.
Mean menace abounds around booming sound.
Hear the ever-evil, bellicose beast, thudding, thumping,
rumbling, grumbling amidst mystery-suffused skies.
Revile that curmudgeonly, bull-bolshie bully, while his hoar
haar shroud devours evanescent light.
How rowdily he endeavours to doom cowardly, cowed
crowds!
Scowling, growling, snarling, sneering; the diabolical
misanthrope vents sinister dins into drifting,
jackdaw-black dark.
Still instilling spine-tingling terror, those twin princes of
quintessential malice conduct ruinous reigns in
intimidating fusion.
The abrasive brace spits aerial, aural, oral spite.
Epitomising ill-will, they malignly espy all through

Mark Lyndon

morose-tinted spectacles.
It is chaos's catharsis.
Pray, quail not before that plunderous, two-fisted
charge.
Quell their blustering, blistering, bomb blast bombast.
Quake nevermore afore fear-fetched trepidation.
Quash lachrymose timorousness, lest zest looks lost.
Corral courage, garner fervour.
Defiantly face fierce adversity.
Indomitable; stare back into the stormy eye of maleficence.
Hamstrung no longer by insidious angst, take trenchant
strides within an allegory meteorological and greet
sprinkled, dawn sunshine when its triumphal glints wink
awake once more.

A Turn For The Verse

All the wistful while, softly percussive waves weave and
slosh ashore.
Their mellow music infuses me, enthuses me, as a
halcyon day's luminescence inexorably surrenders,
sinking in glow-motion to nestle upon nigh-on night.
Diurnal battles 'twixt twin eternal protagonists take a
turn for the verse.
Scanning our cerulean horizon within infinitesimally
dimming light, my mood transmogrifies like the moon.
With each imperceptibly darkening second, puissant
passion's quintessence multiplies exponentially, gushing
torrentially, rushing around this rampant mind of mine.
Imaginary sandman, send me, send me, into transcendent,
other-worldly invisibility, where lives make-believe.
For, only in an unseen realm, where dream-laced
darkness abides, can I discover a mist-lost lover from
yesteryear, amidst nirvana.

Gilded Gower

Half-hidden by angel-hair haar, an old man, in the leaf-fall
of his life, meanders along labyrinths of bracken-fringed
paths and gazes at the nascent wonder of a glistening
seascape.
All but alone, that lark-early bay tripper scuffs beach
detritus and scrunches percussively across a symmetrical
ring of shingle, towards lapping ripples on the slumberous
shore.

Bliss is his vista.

A mellifluous stream trickles seaward, hop-scotching nimbly
o'er bobbling pebbles within Gower's ubiquitous
magnificence.
'Neath serene skies at sunrise,
a hushed tide glides to greet gold-flecked sands.
The horizon, a coal-black hearth, is gently kindled by rosy-
red rays of fiery life, as a somnolent sandman sidles
unseen into the gloaming.
Faintly silhouetted boats wobble upon jiving briny, their
flapping sails inaudible in faraway waves.
Maudlin gulls call and spiral in misty invisibility, swooping to
feast, beacon beaks agape.
Bathing in refracted glory, amid a transient rock pool,
surreal sea creatures plop and gurgle.
Biplane bees zoom in incessant sorties of aeronautical
wizardry.
Exquisite flowers awake and unfurl yawning petals to drink
chinks of poking sunlight.

Mark Lyndon

Stratospheric trees are blessed and burnished in this sublime, timeless place.

Atop a vertiginous dune, an antediluvian castle evokes atavistic scenes of gallant knights from bygone days.

Here, as phantasmagorical clouds drift in ethereal imagery, the fantastical is possible.

Tranquility ever abides in this coastal idyll, where fears are sea-caressed and dissipate at dawn.

Make-believe stirs in crepuscular stillness, as a sanguine ingénue wanders through a gulping cave, then morphs into a magical mermaid.

Only dreamers can hear the silent, twilit departure of intangible night as it slides elsewhere in anonymity.

Only the romantic can feel the distant, thunderous roars of hill-old dragons in cliff-hanging woods.

Only the imaginative can see the far-fetched moon man within his crescent of iridescence as he bids adieu to disappearing stars.

Only the meditative can marvel at that infinite firmament and revel in the splendour of fore.

Appear To Disappear

Listen to little, acrobatic crickets, springing insistently
into zingy existence at amorous summer's behest.
Hypnotic is the rhythmic seduction of their musical
selection.
Praying for prey, a really ugly, yet regally beautiful frog
furtively flips out the forked lightning that is his tongue.
Amidst a cacophonous burst of popping, silver-bauble
bubbles, this prince of amphibians slowly plops into the
pond and appears to disappear in onomatopoeia.

A dapper crowd of darkly armoured crows struts and
flaps, repetitively scouring the ground, pecking
percussively with dagger beaks, in an incessant search
for sustenance.
As dusk nears, night-black bats stir and whirl, with
sinister invisibility, within the rustling canopy.
Though tragically oblivious to this spell-binding spectacular,
these flitting silhouettes are magically masterful in their
twirling world nocturnal.

Mark Lyndon

Tweet Nothings

Cupid's twanging bow unleashes a swishing brace of
unerring arrows which soar across benighted skies,
setting ire afire.
That newly love-struck couple cuddles and canoodles,
entwined as winsome one, entranced by every nuance
of nascent romance.
Peace and piquant passion begin to burgeon within the
smitten.
Euphoria is kindled, till sparkling iridescence dances
amid blazing, anthracite eyes.
Trapped by pure rapture, the sated besotted seem
oblivious to ubiquitous but inconspicuous others milling
invisibly in their pulsating midst.
Love, that most capricious of highs, holds our sensuous
paramours willingly captive, while they gaze through the
glazed prism of its prison.
Its seductive power is all-enthralling.
It is as exclusive as it is elusive and imbues the beautifully
bewitched with soupçons of insouciance.
Tenacious is that indescribably delicious drug's
inescapable grip on delirious addicts.
Such enigmatic magic is more precious than platinum,
more potent than plutonium.
Pray that this lustre lasts as these elated lovebirds swirl
skywards in golden rings of symbolism.
Hear harmony here, inside dulcet tunes, as mellifluous
beloveds tweet dream-weaved duets for eternity.

Gwion Iqbal Malik

Iqbal was born in London to a Welsh mother and East-African Asian father (Kenya). From the age of three he has lived in South Wales and currently lives and works in Swansea as a Probation Officer.

Iqbal is an experienced performance poet and created the 'Spoken Word Swansea' YouTube channel to showcase and promote local poets.
His work has been published in Welsh poetry magazines, including 'Red Poets' and 'Roundyhouse'. and as part of a selective publication, '6', by 'Moonstone Press'.

Iqbal's poetry draws on sharp political and social observations and embraces a wide range of writing styles.

In 2015 Iqbal published his first poetry collection, 'Titans', which is available from the author.

Gwion Iqbal Malik

The Pugilist

The first word I learnt -
was pain.

Marched up to me like a drunken bully.
An old-school Pugilist bobbing and weaving.

And it caught me. More than once.

Had me reeling.
Kissing the canvas.
A bare-knuckled bum -
biting and brawling.

'Till I found my fists. Learnt to fight.
Broke bones of my own.

And didn't stop 'till I was done.

Now it's knives or guns. '9-barrels' burning -
while the chambers whistle and whirl.

Lead tearing into the town.
Rattlesnakes watching.
Clocks stuck at twelve.

And the last sound of the day?
Gunshots. And the thud of bodies hitting dust.

Then silence...

And the click of boots at the bar.
Where whiskey washes away the pain.

Gwion Iqbal Malik

ALWAYS washes away the pain.

Then you wait.

Like one long western...

Watching the mirrors.
Listening.

Till it happens again.

And again.
And again.

Wishing the tumbleweed would stop,
the piano end,
and the credits finally roll.

Gwion Iqbal Malik

Haiku

DIY With Cameron

Fixed the Cabinet.
Looks amazing in The Sun!
Needed lots of tools!

Not Waving But Drowning

Syrian boy drowns.
Washed up with rubbish on
beach.
Tide finally turns.

NHS

Aneurin Bevan.
Built the NHS like Rome.
A relic now. Ciao.

Potato

Oh sweet potato -
Older than the stars and sun.
Chip off the old block.

Junkies

Listen. The flyer flyers and the plyer plyers. Be it his trade, his wares or his soul. Cos this, this takes you! Takes a whole load of you. Till all you are is holes.

Holes upon holes, upon holes - upon holes.

And most don't see them. They just appear - like symptoms in our peripheral vision. Never quite in focus.

'Til we think broken is best or up is down or something. A sort of madness. Like a slow sickness taking hold of you.

And it's not new. We've been here before. Not just once. Round and round and round we go - like a non-stop merry-go-round. "The finest minds of our generation destroyed by madness" - remember? And you don't have to be a Ginsberg to get that!

We're just ticking time-bombs. Distortions of people.

Even life doesn't recognise us. Not cos we're bad - but cos we're mad. I mean, what organism anywhere poisons itself for a laugh! For fun.

It's like we're waiting for God or something to hit the 'magic button' to make it alright. But it's not alright! It's very far from being alright!

See, no-one loves. Not now. I mean, they love things or places or flash cars where they bury themselves, like one long funeral procession - hearse after hearse.

Gwion Iqbal Malik

Lives zig-zagging into nothingness.
A great neon orgy of nothingness.
Industrial people living industrial lives - churned out on one
long conveyer-belt of bullshit.
A never-ending supply of manufactured men and
manufactured women - trained like pigs to bark like dogs.

Soulless little mannequins dressed like dolls. Following
fashion or fame - whatever that means. Pre-programmed
to perform the worst, not the best.

And if we aren't all nearly dead, we're all very actually dead.

Dead dolls in dead houses living dead lives.

Maybe that's why we're here. In dingy rooms and dingy
bars. To down a few drinks or smoke a few smokes. To
gorge ourselves on everything but hope. Cos there's none
left. We cut that out. Cut out our own hearts in some bizarre
ritual. To sacrifice ourselves for money and madness.

Now we're just junkies. Sad little smack-heads trying to get
high one way or another.

Oh Buttercup

Oh Buttercup, my long lost love,
My love so very true;
I wonder at your gentle face,
Your sweet heavenly hue.

Oh Buttercup, my petalled girl
My field of yellow gold;
For you, my love, I'd give the World,
One moment to behold.

Oh Buttercup, I love thee so,
Your swaying, soulful smile;
I fell for you that summer's day,
A dream now so erstwhile.

Atlantis

There was a day back then I decided to write. To give
myself to the gods and see how high I could fly. And it
wasn't long before fireballs came crashing and lightening
 lit up the World. The silver streaks scorching the skies like
transcendent telegrams from other realms. Unleashed with
Angels and Jinns and other supernatural beings from
universes beyond universes.
This was my moment. My time. And whatever I made,
whatever I magicked from the ether, was mine and mine
alone.

Gwion Iqbal Malik

Pete *

Pete's...Pete! Get me?
He's the best!

He greets me.
Meets me.
Even Tweets me!

Well, he tells me he tweets me sweet tweets.
He prefers Mr Men tweets!

Pete never sends texts.

He'll Fed Ex sweet memes,
then pen free verse -
never Welsh verse,
bless.

He spells swell!
Well jel!
He's excellent!

He vents terms,
stretches genres,
re-sets precepts,
Then, tells me: "clever themes sell themselves!"

He's perfect.

The fresh geezer from gent street!
Never lewd. He's shrewd.
He bleeds serene verse.

The rest?
He jests!

See, we need Pete!
Pete, needs Pete!
Pete needs beer, when he's here.
We need beer when we're here.

Pete engenders tender letters.
Never...'sewer' verse!
Pete tells sex pest creeps: "we need less bell-ends!".
He helps brew the perfect zen centre.

He mends me.
Extends me.
Tells me...verse renders TV senseless.

Cheers Pete!

London

There's flyers on the pavement
Fag ends on the street,
Bobbies out in Brixton
Busting blacks on the beat.

There's druggies in the phone-booth
Shootin' up on smack;
Skin-heads causing trouble
With their Yoon-yun Jacks.

Gwion Iqbal Malik

It's London. It's dirty.
A filthy fuckin' mess -
A fairytale of monsters
Outta Herman Hesse.

There's Fat cats in their Rollers
Hookers sellin' wares;
City kids in Soho
With their stock-market shares.

They'll eat out your liver
And then suck our your brain -
Or Halabja your heart
Like some Saddam Hussein.

Cos they're the new-age pirates
With their cut throat plans -
Jack Sparrows on steroids,
Or evil Jackie Chans....

Drop-kicking their dollars
Like a mental Bruce Lee -
To sinister soundtracks
On some shit MP3.

You don't gotta to be clever -
Just a bit street smart;
To see money is the modern-day
Martial art.

I said, money, is the modern day martial art.

Gwion Iqbal Malik

Candy Crush Kids

We're the 'Candy Crush' kids
With Playstation games,
The X-Box generation
Of fortune and fame.

We're the 'Game of Throne' Gods -
Multiplayer Macbeths,
And our high scores better
Than crystal meth.

We have 'Grand Theft Auto'
And 'Mortal Kombat' nights,
Cos 'Flappy Bird' sucks
With it's low-res bytes.

We're the sci-fi shooters
With nothing to show,
But hollowed-out lives
And a bit of blow.

Anne Pelleschi

Anne hails from Swansea, her life and work have evolved from her Welsh origins.

She has organised major international literary events and an international creative writing competition.

Closer to home she established Dylan Thomas' birthplace as a successful centre celebrating his early life.
Nationally and internationally, she is a performer poet and a regular speaker on Thomas' life.

Anne's work is drawn from her lifetime experiences in which people and place provide centrality to her sense of iterative historical and emotional consciousness.

SWANSEA & GOWER

Beach Cottage Penclawdd

The stolen pobbles
torn from estuarial beds
metamorphosise
as the spell binding key stones
which hold the walls together

Llangennith beach art

Words on vast white sand
sensual, emotional
blistered and ingrained
Dug deep in the long blanched beach
where breakers lap and swallow

The Mumbles

Caught in no man's land
a monolithic young child
in media res
the dogs' snarls are in colour
she hears a dangerous red

Ilston Valley

A bright pink football
caught off side in the river
has lost its wide smile
only expectant eyes show
that there was optimism

Anne Pelleschi

For a mother and son

On sweet lover's day
with the King's bible in hand
they accused her son
Their self-righteous malice
made lies holy and bletted

Not guilty of all
that sacred benediction
Hossana'd tears
on cheeks swathed in innocence
fell unbidden and thankful

Maisie

As they breathed out in thanks,
the world's oceans responded.
Waves unanimously swept away
the cutting edge of worry
and replaced it with the face of you.
Your parents' sigh, your baby cry,
made the world stop and start anew.

Anne Pelleschi

THE KENNET & AVON CANAL

Groundwork

There are fruit trees here
amongst the bramble and vine
the path's new surface
indigestible hard core
of stones disgorged by birds

Affinity

She sits in the shade
with her titian hair and book
she looks so at ease
this modern pre-Raphaelite
united with the river

Life after death

Cobwebs on dead trees
catching life as it passes
on the canal's shore
the frail gossamer spun lace
reflects their ghostly light

After the sunshine

A cyclonic gloom
of thick lidded slug black clouds
and bee stinging rain
back stroking water boatmen
swim to the reeds for shelter

Anne Pelleschi

Coed Cadle

It was the early fifties when the family moved into the
new council estate on the edge of a long, wooded valley.
It was school holidays and the sun was shining, the nine
year old made sure that the Swiss Army Knife was safe
in her pocket and confidently left the house.

Her friend lived on the tail end of the woods, near the old
mine shaft, the young girl knocked and waited .
Her friend's father was a policeman who knew everything
and everyone, nobody liked him. When no-one answered
the door, although puzzled, she decided to go on her own.

She had not gone far down the lane which led to the
derelict mine when she saw him pacing around on the
open ground near the river. She stood stock still and
watched this man, who nobody knew, hammering a white
cross into the ground.
She pulled the map out of her pocket and marked the
spot where the cross was placed, there were many
crosses on the map now. Making sure he'd gone, she
went over to the cross, the grave, which was the same
 as the others they'd found - no name, no date.
She pulled out the cross and hid it. Then an awful
thought hit her - maybe he'd got her friend and she
was the one under there.

She ran back to her friend's house and the father was
home. In one breath, she told him about the man,
the cross and the map.
Meanwhile, back in the utilities office, a civil engineer
could not understand where all his ground markers had
gone.

Anne Pelleschi

AMERICA

Reno Nevada

Waltzing to music
with a cowboy hatted man
smokers place your bets

San Francisco

Happy music plays
a billboard bears a bright smile
Alcatraz watches

Little Cottonwood Canyon

Dead bark off some trees
become ribbons of the past
strung up like totems

Reservation

Navajo nation
this spoil tip is in payment
for your stolen land

Carmel California

Abalone shell
echoing a native's life
hanging on his cross

Anne Pelleschi

Beyond Bournemouth

There will always be a clashing of abandonment and
love on that fossiled memorial strand
For its heady, warm and saline sun gives a ghostly
woman's touch
Where the relentlessly beautiful but broken lined swell
grinds every rock to sand

With shoulders mother coated, past tense eyes and
emotions flanged
Take a pilgrim's route through loss of love and a redundant
wedding band for
There will always be a clashing of abandonment and love
on that fossiled memorial strand

Stone baubles for mum with a deep love heart are
gathered to arms unplanned
apart from one, handpicked for strength, that is chosen
by her son
Where the relentlessly beautiful but broken lined swell
grinds every rock to sand

An artesian well of memories waits inside a love lost
man and
finds release through briny eyes wiped dry, enslaved in
time
There will always be a clashing of abandonment and love
on that fossiled memorial strand

Each journeyman has a labyrinth to give their soul core
strength
Along this mantra beaten track comes emotional
confidence though
There will always be a clashing of abandonment and
love on that fossiled memorial strand
Where the relentlessly beautiful but broken lined swell
grinds every rock to sand

Piazza Purgatorio   Agrigento Sicily

Tears of the saints fell as rain drops on the old town square
where coffee drinkers supped and tourists talked.
Accents that were heard were just as cakes served,
some sweet, others sour
but all sitting closely together as the bells struck the hour
of salvation through purgatory.

The edge of law

The dagger's blade was shown as the law's cutting edge.

It sliced through a life, butchered a hope for peace,
slaughtered a profound belief that the good would always
win.

Nowhere in the tomes of law is there guidance for the
healing or re-stitching of a disembowelled core.

Anne Pelleschi

Swansea through a kitchen window

I have known you all my life, at least I thought I knew you
but suddenly you are in my space, laid out in front of me,
showing a side of you that I have never seen before.

I have only known a piece of you, the pretty public face
of you,
not the standing still yet ever moving rhythm of you.
You remind me of how little I know of me, of you, of us.

Together we are part of this town, apart from this town.
Our difference is the likeness reflected through a window
acknowledging this town, seeing us, showing our oneness

The manacle of conditioning

They were wrapped around me, those unseen weights,
placed there like rocks from the day I was born.
I grew tall in the hope that I could outstretch them.
I learned quickly in the hope that I would outsmart them.

Their rules, my ruler, slowly fell at my feet,
entangling and tethering, riveting and controlling,
hooking me into a back footed dance.
Though I swayed and beat boxed, the rhythm was theirs.

One foot kicked for freedom, the other was bolted down,
not able to walk nor waltz, swing nor sashay,
it accepted that it would forever be this way.

Anne Pelleschi

ENGLISH RIVERS & CANALS

River Chertwell

The evening's sound
on the quiet canal
is a chord suspended
from the Woodstock festival
held only for those who hear

A Young Cormorant

Sculpture like you sit
on the bough of a dead tree
I know your parents
but have never thought of them
as you in the prime of youth

Braunston Tunnel

A long slow darkness
six thousand feet cut by hand
subterranean
imperially measured by
navigational moles

River Thames

In old Clivedon House
while lock gates stand listening
Profumo pounces
the pool becomes a voyeur
watching a minister dive

Anne Pelleschi

PARIS

Montmartre

The hill is smoking
in the fingers of tourists
discovering her
on a map or in a book
pilgrim feet still scorch foot paths

Notre Dame

Stonily chiselled
the arid gargoyles look out
for a sunless day
desiccated prayers for rain
are medievally spouted

Les Invalides

Napoleon one
high status is assured
wrapped in base metals
under a sarcophagus
with ashes of ambition

Moulin Rouge

The cacophony
of percussional raindrops
drench a red windmill
drown unsuspecting pavements
render sails into paddles

Alice describes herself as an 'inadvertent poet who enjoys catching kite-tails of words as they float by'.

She stands knee-deep in a chaotic stream of consciousness and children, temporarily looking up and out to escape earthbound mundanity through her writing. Her work captures observations of people, place, motherhood and madness refracted through the truthful but tactless lens of autism.

Originally a Londoner, Alice travelled via Italy to study at Swansea University in 1998. She married a local man and put down roots in Swansea.

Alice is a performer poet who has also contributed to the Carnival Arts online magazine.

Alice Sullivan

Recognition

Overcoming familiar panic
takes an act of will
as nails dig crescents
in palms already marked
with many moons.
I am split and splintered,
deafened by discord
between my many selves.
Logic explains, articulate,
impenetrable chaos unhearing:
somehow they must find a common ground
to seek elusive peace.
I analyse, explain, justify, defend
but struggle, and fight to feel or comprehend
– until I write.
Until I write the hectic round
spill feeling into verse,
hope to portray
something of the curse.
Clarity through the unknowing cloud
– what is sanity?

Alice Sullivan

Post-op

Fragile, like a tiny bird,
beautiful in its frailty,
translucent, almost,
the only sign of life
a subtle rise, fall, pause –
rise, a reassurance that the heart
still beats beneath.

Tubes crawl like veins
across the pale skin,
traverse the great expanse of sheet
to strange machines
doing the organs' job.

No beeps or garish lights,
merely the gentlest hiss –
a flicker behind the eyelids,
a finger moves, a hair…
and you sleep on.

Alice Sullivan

Journey

Womb-red his face with anger,
plum-puce his balled up fist,
the child evicted from familiar warmth
must take his own first breath.

Furious at his journey,
bloody delays and pain,
the traveller survived despite himself.

Metamorphosis, transition, stasis.
His universe imploded –
and the child was born.

Tree

Cobweb fingers stretching upwards,
lace-patterned,
starkly black against pale-gray sky,
silhouette stencils trace
intricate fretwork,
fractured lens filters
refracted light,
familiar view fragmented
through naked spider branches.
A sliver of silver
breaks through the mist,
sets the branch alight
and warms my view.

Alice Sullivan

Pennard

Out of the deep I breathe to you
by still waters in cool shade.
I am the wind, and calm.

Deep in the woods I walk with you
on oily leaves and muddy boots.
I am the rain, and fresh.

Wild in the wind I laugh with you,
and cross green sands to sheltered streams.
I am the sun, and alive.

Out of deep wells your spirit sings,
opens my heart to all created life.
I am you are in me.

Vignette*

The young woman in the photograph
smiles, waves and tucks an escaping
strand of hair behind her ear,
laughing across the years,
mocking her empty shell
in tonight's tired mirror,
shadowing similarities of
cheekbone, mannerism, brow
only serving to amplify
the distance between the two.
And I wonder if I can clarify
who and where is she now?

Alice Sullivan

Shell-shock

The war is over but my fear lives on,
My foot still throbs and itches,
though my leg is gone.
The guns have fallen silent –
Not so the screams in my dreams:
I see and hear my comrades,
smell the stench of the trench,
feel again the unknown terrors.

Boys with catapults pinging stones
Rattling at my window
take me back to memory's hell.
On a summer Saturday
a cricket ball shatters my cup
and I am back in France.
The shrill of gulls becomes the siren wail.
Bullets, shrapnel, shells
fall shattering the silence.
Comrades fall to the ground
to haunt my dreams no more.

Alice Sullivan

Memory

Cold steel in raging furnace,
blistering anger powerless
to melt or burn away
the metallic taste, sharp, unyielding,
Its cutting edge glistening,
sinister on the blade of my
visceral hate.

Imprisoned by bars of my own making,
hardened to armour,
fossilized by pressing years.
I learned to mask my fury,
lock it deep away.

Hatred's a cancer, eating away
not its object but originator.
Metal encages me,
immutable,
poisoning future hope.

Swift stab and slash,
a voice cried out,
a terrible choice,
I bled real blood.

I long to lay down at last
my heavy rock,
blast it to nothingness
by forgiving me,
released from your
decades-old stranglehold.

Alice Sullivan

Listen!

I like to watch people listening.
Some shut their eyes,
others widen them in
sadness or shock
as words come slowly,
gradually or starkly to life
behind their red-dark lids.
I like to listen open-eyed,
and see how others hear.

Listening makes a poem real.
Sharing with you
gives it new strength.
Before being heard,
it's only a series of words
caught on paper
(whatever and wherever
they need to come to me:
notebook, receipt, napkin, loo-roll!)
to clear my busy brain,
as they flit through the screel.

When I hear my words
fly off the page
in print, or microphone,
or someone else's voice
they live and breathe,
receive new life, become
a living entity in their own right…

and a poem is born.

Nightwatch

Midnight strikes, chimes and
electronically beeps.
You turn away from me,
restless, snoring, deep.
Where do you go in those private journeys
punctuated by cries, snuffles,
an arm flung out
across the vast expanse of desert bed?

Shutting me out with a shoulder,
I can't reach through your pain
to help you orientate
to home or me again.
Beep, beep. Figures glowing green
in semi-conscious darkness.
I stare at you asleep
– and keep your watch.

Unstitched

I found holes where I'd lost the thread,
Gaps in the stitching holding me together,
confused by dropped stitches of memory lapse:
Surely I'm too young to be senile?

I couldn't remember my daughter's name.
Flesh of my flesh, fruit of my womb,
I bore her, I love her, she reminds me of home,
but her name is gone!

We spent hours looking for it, and me,

calling her my childhood name.
She laughed uncertainly, both unsure of the joke.
"But that's you, mama!" she said.
I frightened cried, "I can't find Hannah's name!
Oh, there it is. How strange."

I found my keys in the freezer.
Why is your hat in the fridge?
Whose are the socks in the garden?
When did I start to unhinge?
My mind unravels like the wool
in my kitten crazy bag.

My blankets make sense,
the stitches do as they're told.
When madness creeps upon me
knit one, purl one, knit one, slip –
the hypnotic routine re-anchors me
in the safe of here and now.

My blankets make sense
(oh! Did I say that already?)
holding my mind together
in familiar colour blocks.
Meaning filters through addled synapses
as needles collect dropped connections
and missed stitches
in my erstwhile blanket brain.

Juno

Guilty distress, impotence, fury, love.
A Mother's armoury
railing against unfairness
of accident from above.
Should, would, didn't, couldn't,
why wasn't I there?
Nothing I can change now
but I mind, I cry, I care.
My precious child, I'm sorry.
You won't understand
until you too are a parent –
then give me your hand
across years, and tears, forgive me
for loving you so much
I braved your independence
and now you hurt at my touch.
Sickness, fear, injury and pain
I'd love to remove.
But would I do the same again?
Smother you with protection,
or free you with love?

Tony Webb

Tony is a Swansea born performing poet and singer/songwriter who is an experienced guest performer at festivals and events.

Through his choice and command of words, the earthy and evocative messages within his poetry are crafted into lines of powerful fluidity.

His collection of poetry, prose and lyrics, 'Down a Sparrow lane', has been widely distributed and is still available for purchase.

The Pen

The pen hit the paper
There was more truth in that moment
than anything you ever said or thought.
The impact:
The crease in the cloth.
No conversation could ever reveal what you
conveyed in that instant
No painting.
No poem or song,
could eclipse that movement of hand and intention.

Tony Webb

Snake Song

His venom drawn and spat out.
Nowhere to slither and sin.
Every stone too tall.
The gravel tears his belly.
His eyes are shut with contentment,
ready meat for predators,
the artless ones hiding in the corn.
Drawn to him,
they have been long in slumber.
Now his backbone is scythed,
they descend in shadows.
A flock of vipers, a nest of crows.
He has no instinct to repel.
He is content and they can smell it.

Communist Posters

The first televised war.
Black and white atrocities
brought home to me by a book of posters.
The hammer and sickle.
Machine guns in paddy fields.
The old Vietnamese folk song:
'Women must fight, too,
when the country is under attack.'

The six o'clock news,
before colour had arrived.
Those aerial shots.
Clouds or napalm?
We just could not tell.

And there in the posters book,
the role of women,
wives and mothers,
workers and fighters.

Tony Webb

World of Lies

We spoke the truth
and it cleansed us.
But to exist naked was not our desire.
The frankness crushed us.
World of Lies.

And every 'How are you?', speared us.
The second question in every telephone conversation.
'What I was really ringing you for....'
World of Lies.

And soon, every lie became the truth.
And we maintained.
And we prevailed.
World of Lies.

Tony Webb

Sideshow

Let us end this sideshow
before the clowns come on,
I don't have to suffer those antics now

Remember how they were dragged out
on every bank holiday, on television
after the vexing acrobats?

We were supposed to laugh
but those stumbling idiots frightened me
We children, already weary of sparring parents

I am the sideshow now,
locked in my caravan, awaiting my prompt
Whilst you spin your last pirouette

Tony Webb

Brambles (for Anna)

'Now it is Spring, we must!', she demanded
Then she hacked the brambles
And, with her daughters in tow,
She resented the sap that fed the thorns.
Hacking and cutting,
some blood was drawn,
not the first that year.

Her elder was joyous with this power,
to snap and cut the rose bush.
And the younger one too,
just home from her father's house,
ran straight into the garden
to battle with the untamed hedge.

Those merciless incisions.
The first for the mother,
her wrists sore with the conflict.
The fury of those women,
In the garden, that evening.

The Cadet

What entranced the boy?
The lad in grey and blue.
His mischievous mates?

They enticed him to join!
To hang from the rafters,
to echo their boots on the drill hall's floor.

To pilot a plane
at the age of fifteen.
Nebulous thrills,
threading the clouds.

He has awards now,
for Rugby and Rowing
and Cooking and Hygiene.

And guns
and guns,
even for the cooks,
even for the cooks.

Tony Webb

Map of the world

Gifts for you are pointless.
I gave you an atlas.
You smiled,
and showed me your wall with its map of the World,
as big as the World.
Even the smallest town eclipsed the size of my hand.

Its rivers stained the ceiling.
I could have walked from Pole to Pole.
The harvest from that replica could have ended famine.
And you, you soared above its delineations.
Whilst I drowned in its fathoms.

I bought you an atlas.
You smiled.
And showed me your map of the World.
as big as the World.

Anchor

"'Anchor' is a stupid name for your hero!"
 Jordan stood there and continued his rant:
 "'Anchor?', 'Anchor?', have you ever met anyone called
that? is it supposed to be profound? Oh, I know
- a deep anchor! What will you call him for short - Hank?"

Tom replied, "Anchor is my middle name, it is a family
name. My mother lumbered me with it."
"And 'Anchor' is, of course you, I suppose - you are the
anti - hero."
"Thank you, Jordan, with a name like that you've got
nothing to joke about"
They sat there in Karl's front room, jabbing each other
with charming insults. Karl, Tom's landlord, was at a
football match, so they got stuck into his brandy.

Tom let rip at his younger friend, "Look at you, in a time
warp!. Tweed jacket, ginger beard and cord trousers....
and that fake electric fag, for God's sake! Where's your
 felt hat? I've written 22,000 words already. That's more
than you've managed, unless you count 'see me'
or 'could do better'!".

Jordan hit back where he knew it would hurt,
 "I've been published in the Guardian, mate!".
"All fourteen lines of it", laughed Tom.
"They also printed one by Caitlin Williams, you know,
her who refers to the Atlantic as 'the Pond'".

"She's good, come on!", argued Jordan.

Tony Webb

"No! She's an effing mixture of George Formby
and Pam Ayres when she plays that bloody ukulele
 - and that crap poem about burning her ex-husband
on a totem pole. What tripe!",replied Tom.

Jordan puffed on his fake fag and said,
 "Hey Tom, these work. They should do fake gin
 bottles with bloody teats for the likes of you."

Jordan stayed for a week.

The first meeting between Tom's new squeeze,
let's call her 'Tasmin' and Jordan, was notable for her
candour.
Earlier, Tom had rung her to request that she take
Jordan to the shops,
 "It's raining, you see and he's tired after his journey."

When she arrived, Jordan looked up pitifully from
behind his beard and brandy.
 "Just get up off your arse", Tasmin told him, "I've been
working all day".
This was the first time they had met.

Tom heard the front door open. Karl was back from
the match, Tom heard him muttering "Never again".

"Yes", thought Tom, " never again!"

Glossary

INDEX

INDEX

INDEX

Dedications from:

David Churchill

I direct what I write to Rhiannon and my sons, to whom I owe thanks for so many things

Teifion Hughes

I was small when my parents moved to a wooded world where I could never be found I should have thanked them for the words.

Rebecca Lowe

Special thanks to: Rob, Stephanie, Mum and Dad

Mark Lyndon

I dedicate these poems to my late father, Tom Lyndon, who passed on his passion for 'bard' language to me

Anne Pelleschi

I am thankful to have been born in Swansea and become a part of its mortar. My sons, Tom and Jack give me the internal support that every mother needs.

Alice Sullivan

Thank you Dith, Becky and Lisa for daring me to write again and to Dai for always believing in me.

Tony Webb

I wish to thank Nia, Christian, Jackson and Theresa for their support and inspiration.

The writers in this anthology offer thanks to John Collins for the idea of setting up what has now become Talisman Poetry.

Thanks to Tino for embracing the spirit of spoken word evenings with patience, good humour and enthusiasm.

Talisman Poetry is part of a strong network of poetry groups in the local and wider area and offer thanks, in particular, to;

HOWL; Mad as Birds; Poets on the Hill; and to poetry friends in Neath, Pontardawe and Carmarthen.

Amicus poeticae